Neighbors at Work

by Susan Markowitz Meredith

This is my neighborhood.
I live here.
I have many neighbors.

This is Mr. Brill.
He works in the grocery store.
I got milk and bread here today.

Mr. Wong works in the library.
He helps me get books to read.
Today I got a new book.

Mrs. Stern is a mail carrier.
Do you see the letters
in her mailbag?
Today she has a letter
for me!

Mr. Castro works in the park.
He cuts the trees.
I like to play ball in the park.

Ms. Perez cuts my mom's hair in her shop.
She cuts my hair, too.

Mr. Spano works in the pizza shop.
I eat here with my mom and dad.
They like pizza. I like spaghetti.

I like my neighbors.